Fleas, Knees and Hidden Elephants

SPIKE MILLIGAN

Fleas, Knees and Hidden elephants

Jacket and inside illustrations by
PHILIP HOPMAN

BOXTREE

First Published in Great Britain in 1994 by
Boxtree Limited, Broadwall House, 21 Broadwall,
London SE1 9PL

Text copyright © Spike Milligan Productions Ltd., 1994
Illustrations copyright © Philip Hopman, 1994

Book and jacket design by Design 23
Jacket and inside illustrations by Philip Hopman

10987654321

Printed in Great Britain by The Bath Press, Avon

A CIP catalogue entry for this book is available from the British
Library.

ISBN: 0 7522 0832 2

Contents

Timothy Nerp

Timothy Nerp was a terrible Twerp
A terrible Twerp was he
He wore his trousers back to front
To keep out the raging sea
He wore his socks both inside out
To stop the rising damp
He filled his boots with mustard
To stop the dreaded cramp
He wore his Trilby upside down
To try and catch the rain
Then every day at half past one
He'd start all over again.

Skin Deep

I think that I am lovely
Despite a broken nose
You can detract from it
By wearing fancy clothes
I think I am beautiful
Although I have cross-eyes
You can detract from that as well
By wearing fancy ties
I think I am beautiful
Even though I've got big ears
I cover them with blankets
When anyone appears.
I think I am beautiful
Although my legs are thin
If people want to see them
I say my legs aren't in
If some folk say I'm ugly
As some folk certainly will
I get out my rotweiler
And say kill kill kill

Hidden **E**lephant

Splitty splitty splat!
What was that?
Splitty splitty splat!
Was it a rat?
Can a rat go splitty splitty splat?
No! Then can a cat?
No! Cats only go miaow
Don't ask me how
Can a cow go splitty splitty splat?
No cows go moo
That's what they do
Splitty splitty splat!
Heavens! It's somewhere in my flat!
Got it! It's an elephant under my hat!

Trousers

Somehow my trousers have got bent
Right in the middle there's a dent
I tried to straighten them on the
floor
But somehow they ended up next
door
I went for a walk with these
trousers bent
They took me to a place in
Kent
With my trousers back to
front, away I darted
Only to end up where
I started.

12

Terence Blatt

Terence Blatt
Wore bells on his hat
To keep the wolves at bay
With a gun by his side
He went for a ride
In his one horse open sleigh
A wolf pursued him
As snow began to fall
It ate him up bells and all
Oh dear Terence what terrible luck
The wolf of course did'nt give a fig

13

The Dancer

He danced with a monkey
  He danced with a cat
  And he danced with a man
  In a big black hat
  He danced with a Muslim
  He danced with a Jew
  And he danced with a Chinaman
  Six foot two
  Then he took all his clothes off
  And he danced all day
  That's when they came
  And took him away.

Tiger

There came a tiger trailing me
So I climbed up a banana tree
The tiger wouldn't go away
So, where I was, I had to stay
I threw a banana on his head
Lo and behold, it struck him dead.
So if you don't want to come to any harmer
Always carry a spare banana.

Vivat Regina

He was a brave captain of a ship
Was Captain Roger Hyde
He ruled with a rod of iron
Some men broke down and cried
He used to flog his sailors
Many of them died
So the crew tied up the Captain
And threw him over the side
They cheered him as he floated
Out with the noon day tide
Even though he was sinking fast
"God Save The Queen", he cried
So God saved the Queen but the
Captain died.

Hi Wire

There was a tight rope walker,
Who let his wire go slack.
For this indiscretion,
He came down on his back
You see that slack rope walkers
Are very very rare
And only where the rope is slack
Will you find them there.
Now, these slack rope walkers,
Think high ropes are unsound
That's why you'll only find them
With both feet on the ground.

Piffed

I piffed at my mother
I piffed at my dad
"Will you stop that piffing
It's driving us mad!"
I piffed at my mistress
The next day at school
I piffed and I piffed
The silly old fool.
I piffed at Willy
I piffed at Bert
And I piffed at the tail
Of my grandad's shirt
Oh I piffed and I piffed
Oh I piffed everywhere.
Then I piffed at the Queen
So there - so there.

Tiger

I'm hunting for a tiger skin
Here's the jungle, I go in
Into view the tiger came
So very carefully, I took aim
The tiger gave a sudden cough
And when he did, his stripes fell off.

Hello Sailor

So I am a jolly sailor
  And I am off to sea
  All the family gather there
  To wave good-bye to me
  Some wave from the window
  Some wave from the door
  Some stand on the toilet seat
  Some lay on the floor
  Some wave from the table
  Some wave from the chair
  Some of them climb on the roof
  And wave goodbye from there
  For all this frantic waving
  I cannot care a lot
  Because mu dear dear reader
  I hate the bloody lot.

The Hills Are Alive

Climb every mountain
Ford every stream
Follow every rainbow
Till you find you're knackered.

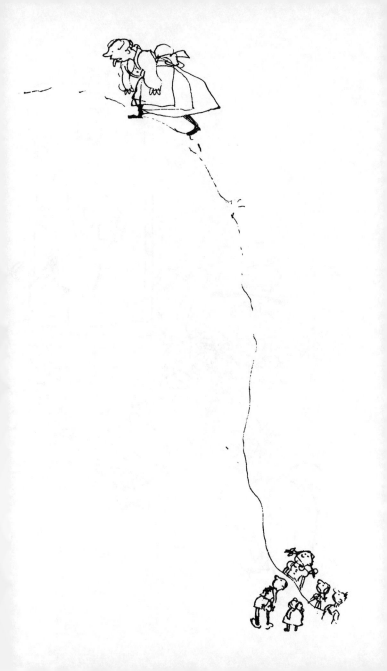

Never Never

Never force cats to wear hats
It'll stop them catching rats
Never put a dog in trousers
It could stop them guarding our houses
You must never put a duck in slacks
It would surely stop his flow of quacks
Never force a goose into a gown
It would only go honk and then drown.
You must never cross a chicken's leg
Unless you want some funny shaped eggs
Never put a monicle on a rooster
Or he will think he's Bertie Wooster
These are things you mustn't do
Now off to the vets with all of you.

Dali Lama

The Dali Lama
Wore half a pyjama
When he went to bed
The other half
He ate for a laugh
And this disease could spread

The Dali Lama
Wore half a pyjama
Red and white and blue
The other half
He burnt on a staff
Now this would never do.

The Dali Lama
Wore half a pyjama
Eating jam and bread
The other half
He fed to a calf
He's getting no better, they said.

The Donkey

Hee-haw said the donkey
He who said the mule
He me said the donkey
That's who you silly fool.

Hip**p**o

The hippopotamus
Is not like a lot of us.
He can't tell
The Queen from a
bus
He can't tell
when
It's half
past
eight
That is
why
He's always
late
When it is
The first of
May
To him it's just
Another day
Such an ignoramus
Is the hippopotamus

Child's Prayer

Can you hear me God?
Can you? Can you?
Do you have big ears God
Do you? Do you?
Do they help you listen in
Or is it because the walls are thin
What's it like being God
Does it make you ever feel odd
Up there can you get apple-pie
How can you eat it up so high
Please can I see you God
Only just a peep!
If you're not here by 8 o'clock
I'm going off to sleep

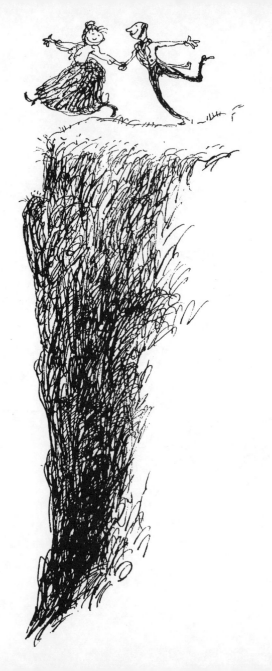

My Love and I

My love and I
A-wickling go
Whickle whackle woo

My love and I
A-wickling went
Tickle Ickle too

My love and I
A-wickling did
Bickle backle biff

My love and I
Wickled away
And both fell over a cliff

B_{ig} HEAD

My name is Fred
I've got a big head
With my head on the pillow
It collapses the bed
One day I went to buy a hat
The man said help!
We could never fit that
So now when I go out of doors
On my head I wear a chest of drawers
If I want to see what's behind or before
I throw out the clothes and open a drawer

Donkey

Do not touch that donkey, mam
Mam I'm warning you
That donkey has a disease
Called Itchy dangle do
If you touch that donkey mam
You'll start to go bright green
Even reaching parts of you
That you have never seen
So then my dear madam
A warning to the few
If you get near that donkey
He'll do it over you.

Il Papa

The Pope arose at 6pm
And said his morning prayer
When he'd had his breakfast
He said another there
Then just before shaving
He blessed his razor blade
Then a prayer of hope
For his shaving soap
And the place where it was made
Then he prayed to St Theresa
To straighten the Tower of Pisa
While wearing his white fur capel
He blessed the Sistine Chapel
When saying grace before meals
He fell backwards head over heals
He said you see my dearest God
You made me such a clumsy sod.

The Purtakon

See there the Purtakon
  See the slender girth
  And the scarlet yondel
  Grown like that since birth.
  See how the Purtakon
  Goes gargle-argle goo
  Best stand back
  Or he'll attack
  And squirt it over you.

Now hear how the Purtakon
  Is making such a din
  I'll have to shout
  Let's all get out!
  The way that we got in.

Knees (song)

You've got to have knees
You've got to have knees
They're the things that take stock when
you sneeze
You've got to have knees
You've got to have knees
They only come in twos but never threes
You've got to have knees
You've got to have knees
In the winter fill them up with anti-freeze
You've got to have knees
You've got to have knees
Famous for having them are bees
You've got to have knees
You've got to have knees
If you want to see mine, say please
You've got to have knees
You've got to have knees
They help you run away from falling
trees
Knees. Wonderful knees!

Ponk a Loo

It's Ponk a Loo - ho Ponk a Loo
That's the thing the Chinese do
They go Ponk a Loo out doors
And sometimes on the bathroom floors
They say it causes no offence
But difficult when crowds are dense
So Ponk a Loo Ponk a Loo
The Chinese do it - why don't you?

The Lion

If you're attacked by a lion,
Find fresh underpants to try on.
Lay on the ground, keep quite still,
Pretend that you are very ill
Keep like that, day after day
Perhaps the lion will go away.

My Nanny

I had a Nanny six foot three
She nearly was the death of me
Through roaring traffic she'd push
my pram
Down my throat my food she'd ram
It made her ecstatically happy
To never ever change my nappy
So it shouldn't surprise you a bit
That I grew up a bit of a shit.

The Leg

The other day I gave a cough
There and then my leg fell off
A policeman gave it a stamp
And said "You cannot leave it there "
I took it to a doctor who said
I'm sorry but this leg is dead
I was shocked into grieving
Then I heard the leg still breaking!
When I knew it wasn't dead
I rushed it to a hospital bed
It was stitched back on by Doctor Hay
But facing alas, the other way
Now when I walk I have found
I only go around and around.

Horses

Horses for courses
Who said that?
He must be talking
Through his hat
A horse is something
I never ate
First it wouldn't fit
On the plate.
Supposing, it was
Under done
He'd give a snort
And away he'd run.
Leaving you with
Just potatoes and peas
Not much of a meal
If you please
What was supposed to be your dinner
Could be next years
Derby Winner.

Money

Money is the root of all evil
That's what people say
Some say it in the night
Others in the day
Some people say it when they're near
Some say it far away.
In England you don't see money
Only where it's been
Mine's been gone a long time now
God save the Queen

Fleas

I have two radio controlled-fleas
I direct them as I please
Right now they're biting Auntie Flo
Somewhere where it doesn't show
The fleas will next get Uncle Fred
The moment that he gets in bed
Then there was Auntie Nelly
They both got her in the belly
Next they got my Uncle Art
They got him in a private part
Finally my Dad and Mum
They were bitten on the knees.

* see Knees poem